THE NEW
BELIEVER'S
HANDBOOK

MY HEALTHY CHURCH®
Equipping Spirit-Empowered People

02-0272

Acknowledgements

The New Believer's Handbook is adapted from the best-selling *Now What?* by Ralph W. Harris.

My Healthy Church would like to thank Randy Hurst for allowing us to include excerpts from *Following Christ* (formerly *Guidance for Life*), and Rebecca Gullion for adapting the two resources into a new tool for new Christians.

Also available—

The New Believer's Friend Handbook (02-0280) provides answers for the Bible study questions on the following pages. Designed to be used by a Christian friend who partners with a new believer, this resource would also be beneficial to you if you are using this handbook for self study.

Scripture taken from the HOLY BIBLE, NEW INTERNATIONAL VERSION®. NIV®. Copyright© 1973, 1978, 1984 by International Bible Society. Used by permission of Zondervan. All rights reserved.

6th printing 2014

ISBN 978-1-62423-051-6

Printed in United States of America

CONTENTS

CONGRATULATIONS!

You just made the best decision of your life by accepting Jesus as your Lord and Savior. But what happens now? Where do you go from here?

The upcoming weeks are key as you begin a new life as a Christian, or follower of Jesus Christ and His teachings. Just like anything new, there will be some clear differences from the old. This handbook will help you understand those differences and get you started in the right direction. It gives guidance for the next eight weeks, with a chapter designed for each. Read the chapters carefully, and follow the helps given.

One of the first things to do in this new life is obtain a Bible and read some of it every day. The Bible is God's written message to all people. It helps us better understand who God is and how to make Him part of our lives. Use a Bible written in a modern translation, such as the New International Version, *New Living Translation*, or New King James Version. Bibles can be purchased at a book or discount store.

You should also find a good Christian friend to help guide you in your new life. This friend can help you answer the questions you will have along the way, and offer support when you need it. This Christian friend can also help you choose a good Bible translation.

Each chapter of this handbook includes some basic teaching about being a Christian, a daily Bible reading plan, and Bible study questions. The Bible reading plan will walk you through a short portion of the Bible named after its writer, Mark. It is found about two-thirds of the way through the Bible in a section called the New Testament. Mark recounts the good news about the life of Jesus Christ.

The Bible study questions at the end of each day's reading will take very little time, and they will help you understand how to effectively study the Bible. The total time needed for the Bible study each day is less than half an hour.

Do your best and God will help you!

WHAT HAPPENED TO ME?

Just what has happened to you exactly?
That's a good question, and an important one.
Knowing what happened and what it means will
help you best begin your new life as a Christian.

It may have happened in a church, in your home,
anywhere. Someone may have been with you,
or perhaps you were by yourself. Maybe you felt
something missing in your life, or you turned to
Jesus for help in a desperate situation. One way
or another, you asked Him to be a part of your life.

Now, what does it all mean? To put it
simply, two things have happened:

    1. Jesus has become your Savior.

    2. You have become a child of God.

We call this salvation. Perhaps someone
has already said that now you are saved. Maybe
you wonder what that means. Saved from what?
Why did you need to be saved? Three things are
important for you to know:

    1. You were a sinner.

    2. You could not save yourself.

    3. Only Jesus could save you.

The Bible says, "All have sinned" (Romans 3:23).
Sin is doing anything that you know is wrong, and
everyone, except Jesus, has done this. The Bible

also says, "The wages of sin is death" (Romans 6:23). This kind of death is spiritual and eternal.

No one can be saved from this death by good works, church membership, or trying to be a moral person. The only way to be saved from the penalty of sin is to somehow provide payment.

Jesus provided the only sufficient payment for sin by dying on a cross many years ago. He took upon himself the punishment for all sin. When you asked God to forgive your sins and believed Jesus died for you, God accepted you for Jesus' sake, your sins were forgiven, and Jesus became your Savior.

But something else has happened. You have become a child of God.

A child of God? What does that mean? Look at it this way. When you were born as a baby, you received natural life from your parents. Because of this, you are like them and have many of their characteristics.

When Jesus became your Savior, He brought you new life, spiritual life, life from God. The Bible calls this the new birth (John 3:3). By your first birth, you became a child of your earthly parents; by your new birth, you have become a child of God.

This is important! You now have two natures: (1) the old nature you received when physically born the first time and (2) the new nature you received with the new, spiritual birth. Jesus Christ is now living with you by His Holy Spirit. The Holy Spirit is God, living inside Christians, giving them power to live like Jesus. You are living a new life with a new nature that draws you away from sin and to Jesus.

As far as your first, or natural, birth is concerned, you may be an adult, a youth, or a child. But as far as your new, or spiritual, birth is concerned, you are a newborn. You have received a new life, but it's just beginning.

During these next few weeks your new nature will begin to grow stronger as you develop good habits. These are very important weeks as you set the patterns to base the rest of your life on.

Next is your Bible reading plan and study questions for this first week. These will help you develop a habit of reading and studying the Bible.

WEEK ONE • DAY ONE
Bible Reading & Study Questions from Mark 1:1–8

1. What did the prophet Isaiah say John would do? (Mark 1:2,3)

2. What two things did John do to prepare the way for Jesus? (Mark 1:4)

3. What kind of baptism did John preach and perform? (Mark 1:4)

4. What did John say Jesus would baptize with? (Mark 1:8)

WEEK ONE • DAY TWO
Bible Reading & Study Questions from Mark 1:9–20

1. What was the role of the Holy Spirit at Jesus' water baptism? (Mark 1:10)

2. What was God's response to Jesus' water baptism? (Mark 1:11)

3. What did Jesus say a person should do to prepare for the kingdom of God? (Mark 1:15)

4. What did Jesus tell Simon and Andrew He would make them? (Mark 1:17)

WEEK ONE ▪ DAY THREE
Bible Reading & Study Questions from Mark 1:21–34

1. Why were the people amazed at Jesus' teaching? (Mark 1:22)

2. What did the evil spirit know about Jesus? (Mark 1:24)

3. What did Simon's mother-in-law do after Jesus healed her? (Mark 1:31)

4. Who did the people bring to Jesus to be healed? (Mark 1:32)

WEEK ONE ▪ DAY FOUR
Bible Reading & Study Questions from Mark 1:35–45

1. What time of day did Jesus pray? (Mark 1:35)

2. When the man with leprosy asked if Jesus was willing to heal him, what did Jesus say? (Mark 1:41)

3. What did the man with leprosy do after Jesus
   healed him? (Mark 1:45)

WEEK ONE ▪ DAY FIVE
Bible Reading & Study Questions from Mark 2:1–12

1. Whose faith did Jesus respond to in healing the
   paralytic man? (Mark 2:5)

2. What did Jesus say to the paralytic man?
   (Mark 2:5)

3. Why did Jesus' statement to the paralytic man
   upset the teachers of the Law? (Mark 2:6)

4. What did healing the paralytic man prove?
   (Mark 2:10)

5. If only God can forgive sins (Mark 2:6) but Jesus
   also has the power to forgive sins (Mark 2:10),
   what do these verses tell us about Jesus?

1. Who did Jesus spend time with? (Mark 2:15)

2. Who did Jesus compare sinners to? (Mark 2:17)

3. Who did Jesus compare himself to? (Mark 2:17)

4. Who else did Jesus compare himself to?
   (Mark 2:19)

1. What were Jesus' disciples doing on the
   Sabbath? (Mark 2:23)

2. What person did Jesus use as an example to
   justify His disciples' actions? (Mark 2:25)

3. What did Jesus say to defend His disciples?
   (Mark 2:27)

4. Who is Lord of the Sabbath? (Mark 2:28)

WHERE DO I GO FROM HERE?

Week 1 established that you're a spiritual newborn, with need of maturity. So where do you go from here?

It is tragic when, because of a physical affliction, a child fails to mature and mentally remains a baby for life. It's even more tragic when a person becomes a child of God through salvation and then fails to mature spiritually.

This doesn't have to happen to you. As you follow these suggestions, you can begin to become a strong, mature Christian.

First of all, remember that your spiritual life comes from Jesus, the Son of God. "God has given us eternal life, and this life is in his Son. He who has the Son has life; he who does not have the Son of God does not have life" (1 John 5:11,12).

Receiving life is not enough; you must nourish that life. When a baby is born in the natural, it will die unless its parents (or someone) take care of it. They must feed and nourish the baby's physical life so it will grow.

This is also true in relation to your new spiritual life. If you feed it, it will grow; if you neglect it, it will die. "Like newborn babies, crave pure spiritual milk, so that by it you may grow up in your salvation" (1 Peter 2:2).

It's as simple as that. Your spiritual growth depends on how and what you feed yourself spiritually. Here are some keys that will help you grow.

READ THE BIBLE

In week 3 we'll talk more about the Bible. Your use of the Bible will determine the kind of Christian you will be. This is why we've provided a Bible reading plan for your first few weeks. Make a habit of reading the Bible every day.

PRAY

In week 4 we'll talk about various kinds of prayer and how to pray effectively. The simplest way to describe prayer is that it is talking to God and letting Him talk to us. Make time every day to pray.

For many people, the best time to pray is the first thing in the morning, before starting daily activities. Talk to Him as you would to a friend— He is your best Friend and you can talk to Him anytime. Don't worry about using the right words. God is more concerned with your attitude than with your vocabulary.

WITNESS TO OTHERS

Tell others about what has happened to you. A witness is someone who tells others about something he or she has learned personally. If you have learned that Jesus can forgive, let others know about it too.

Witnessing is saying and doing things that point people to Jesus. Let everyone know how wonderful your new Friend can be to him or her. Witnessing will make you a stronger Christian.

ATTEND CHURCH REGULARLY

If you take a live coal from the fireplace and put it by itself, it will soon go out. But, it can keep its heat and even ignite other materials if it is kept in the fireplace near other coals.

In the same way, Christians need the encouragement of other Christians, which comes by attending church. Listening to the pastor and other mature Christians preach and teach the Word of God, praying with others, singing together, making Christian friendships—these will help you grow (Hebrews 10:25).

BE OBEDIENT

When God asks you to do or not to do something, obey quickly. Jesus is your Master as well as your Savior. Here is a good question to ask when deciding what is right or wrong: Will this be pleasing to God? Make this the ruling factor in all you do or say.

Spiritual maturity does not depend on how long you have been saved. It depends on how committed you are to doing what it takes to become spiritually mature.

WEEK TWO • DAY ONE
Bible Reading & Study Questions from Mark 3:1–19

1. What did Jesus ask the Pharisees to help them understand the intent of the Sabbath? (Mark 3:4)

2. What was the Pharisees' problem? (Mark 3:5)

3. Who did the evil spirits recognize Jesus to be? (Mark 3:11)

4. What three duties are mentioned for the twelve apostles? (Mark 3:14)

1. What did the teachers of the law accuse Jesus of? (Mark 3:22,30)

2. What three reasons would prevent Satan from opposing himself? (Mark 3:26)

3. What sins can be forgiven? (Mark 3:28)

4. Who is a part of Jesus' family? (Mark 3:35)

1. What does the "seed" represent? (Mark 4:14)

2. What happens to the "seed" that falls along the path? (Mark 4:15)

3. Why do people who are on "rocky ground" turn away from God quickly? (Mark 4:17)

4. What prevents people who are on "thorny ground" from producing fruit? (Mark 4:19)

5. What type of crop do people who are on "good ground" produce? (Mark 4:20)

WEEK TWO · DAY FOUR
Bible Reading & Study Questions from Mark 4:21–25

1. Where do you put a lamp? (Mark 4:21)

2. Psalm 119:11 indicates we should hide God's Word (the Bible) in our hearts. What does Mark say we should do with God's hidden Word? (Mark 4:22)

3. What two things should we do after hearing the Word of God? (Mark 4:24)

1. What happens to the seed after it is scattered? (Mark 4:27)

2. What is produced? (Mark 4:28)

3. What happens after the grain is ripe? (Mark 4:29)

1. What small seed does Jesus use as an illustration? (Mark 4:31)

2. What happens after the seed is planted? (Mark 4:32)

3. What did Jesus use to teach the crowds? (Mark 4:33,34)

4. What did Jesus do differently with His disciples? (Mark 4:34)

1. What was Jesus doing while on the boat when the storm arose? (Mark 4:38)

2. What did Jesus' disciples ask Him? (Mark 4:38)

3. How did Jesus show His disciples that He cared what happened to them? (Mark 4:39)

4. What did the disciples' fear of the storm indicate? (Mark 4:40)

HOW CAN I UNDERSTAND THE BIBLE?

As mentioned in week 2, reading the Bible is one of the best ways to be fed and help your spiritual growth. It is "able to make you wise for salvation through faith in Christ Jesus. All Scripture is God-breathed and is useful for teaching, rebuking, correcting and training in righteousness, so that the man of God may be thoroughly equipped for every good work" (2 Timothy 3:15–17).

The Bible is often called *the Word* because it is one of God's ways of communicating with us. We use words to express ourselves to others. God uses the Bible to express himself to us. There are five common ways to make the Bible a part of your life.

READ THE WORD

Habits influence our character, and one of the best habits you can have to form good character is to read the Bible every day. The best way to make Bible reading a habit is to establish a regular time and place to do your reading. Repetition and familiarity create habits.

Set a reasonable pace for yourself. Start by reading fifteen minutes a day. Many people find the best time of day is in the morning. Other possible reading times include before going to bed at night or during lunchtime. It's not really important what time of day you choose; it is important that you set aside time in your schedule to read the Bible each day without distractions.

We suggest using a Bible in a modern translation, such as the New International Version, *New Living Translation*, or New King James Version. Use a Bible in which you can underline with a pen and write notes in the margin. See page 80 for suggestions about what to read after you finish reading the Book of Mark.

HEAR THE WORD

Because hearing is another way of receiving the Word of God into your life, it is important that you form the habit of attending church services as often as possible. There you will hear the pastor and other mature Christians preach and teach the Word of God. Taking notes will help you remember what you hear.

STUDY THE WORD

Studying the Bible takes time, but is an extremely valuable exercise for understanding it. For in-depth studying you will need longer time periods, usually an hour at least—perhaps an entire evening when you have a free one.

The Bible is one method God uses to communicate to you. Parts of the Bible can seem unclear and need more study to understand them better. When a passage is unclear, pray and ask God to help you concentrate on, understand, and apply what you are reading. Then try re-reading the passage. If you still have problems, write down the questions so you can ask another Christian.

When you are studying a passage, use the following categorized questions to help you better understand what you are reading.

Intent. What does this passage or verse say? What did the writer mean when it was originally written? Who was it written to? What are the subjects it addresses? How does it apply to you?

Difficulty. What does this verse or passage say that you don't understand? What particular words or phrases make it unclear?

Comparison. What similar thoughts are found elsewhere in the Bible? (The more you study, the more you see common threads throughout the Bible.)

Promises. What blessings and helps are stated or implied? Were they intended for a specific individual or for all people?

Warnings. What warnings do you find? How do these warnings apply to your everyday life?

Commands. What commands are stated or implied for you to obey?

MEMORIZE THE WORD

Memorization of verses is another way to help you use God's Word in your daily life. Also, it is one way to obey the verse, "I have hidden your word in my heart that I might not sin against you" (Psalm 119:11).

Start with some of the verses listed at the end of this handbook. Look at the various parts of the verse you are memorizing to see what each means. Then, notice the important words. For example, in Psalm 119:11 the important words are *hidden*, *word*, and *heart*. Focusing on the important words of the verse will help you memorize it. Memorize the reference as well so you can help others find it.

MEDITATE ON THE WORD

After you have read, heard, studied, and memorized a Bible verse, you have something to meditate (intently think) on. In the spare moments of the day—working around the house, waiting for an elevator, driving down the street—you can clear your mind and meditate on Bible verses you have learned. If you can't sleep at night, try thinking about a verse or passage from the Bible.

WEEK THREE • DAY ONE
Bible Reading & Study Questions from Mark 5:1–20

1. List the four things that describe the man with an evil spirit prior to his meeting Jesus. (Mark 5:3–5)

2. List the three actions of the demon-possessed man after his encounter with Jesus. (Mark 5:15)

3. What did Jesus tell the man to do? (Mark 5:19)

1. How long had the woman been subject to bleeding? (Mark 5:25)

2. What happened immediately after she touched Jesus' clothing? (Mark 5:29)

3. How did Jesus know that someone in the large crowd had touched His clothes? (Mark 5:30)

4. What did Jesus tell the woman? (Mark 5:34)

5. What happened to Jairus's sick daughter before Jesus could arrive? (Mark 5:35)

6. What did Jesus do? (Mark 5:40–43)

7. How old was Jairus's daughter? (Mark 5:42)

WEEK THREE ▪ DAY THREE
Bible Reading & Study Questions from Mark 6:1–6

1. Why were the people in Jesus' hometown amazed about Him? (Mark 6:2)

2. Why were they offended? (Mark 6:3)

3. What amazed Jesus and why couldn't He do many miracles there? (Mark 6:6)

WEEK THREE ▪ DAY FOUR
Bible Reading & Study Questions from Mark 6:7–13

1. What did Jesus give the Twelve authority over? (Mark 6:7)

2. How do we know that Jesus wanted the Twelve to be cared for by the people they ministered to? (Mark 6:8–10)

3. What did the Twelve preach? (Mark 6:12)

1. Why did Herod's wife, Herodias, hold a grudge against John the Baptist? (Mark 6:18)

2. Why did Herod not want to kill John? (Mark 6:20)

3. Why did Herod kill John? (Mark 6:26)

4. How was John executed? (Mark 6:27,28)

WEEK THREE ▪ DAY SIX
Bible Reading & Study Questions from Mark 6:30–44

1. Why did Jesus have compassion on the crowd? (Mark 6:34)

2. Name two ways Jesus showed compassion on the crowd. (Mark 6:34,41–42)

3. How many loaves and fish did Jesus give thanks for? How much food was left over? (Mark 6:38,43)

4. How many men were fed? (Mark 6:44)

WEEK THREE ▪ DAY SEVEN
Bible Reading & Study Questions from Mark 6:45–56

1. What did Jesus do following the feeding of the five thousand? (Mark 6:45,46)

2. What did Jesus do when He saw that the disciples were having difficulty rowing the boat because of the strong wind? (Mark 6:48)

3. What happened as soon as Jesus climbed into the boat? (Mark 6:51)

HOW CAN I PRAY EFFECTIVELY?

If the Bible can be compared to food because it nourishes our spiritual lives, then prayer can be compared to breathing. There are two parts to breathing—inhaling and exhaling. So it is with prayer—talking to God and listening for His response.

The person who says, "I can't find time for prayer," may have a point. Most people have to make time for prayer. A good time to pray regularly is along with your Bible reading. In fact, when something you read stands out, stop for a few moments and pray about it.

One trait of a solid, mature Christian is a consistent prayer life.

WHAT TO PRAY ABOUT

One of your first challenges when learning to pray is knowing what to pray about. Most people think of their family, friends, associates, and personal needs—then in five minutes they have run out of things to say. One way to solve this problem is to focus your prayer on certain topics, a different topic each day. Page 83 of this handbook has suggestions. Another solution is to utilize different kinds of prayer.

KINDS OF PRAYER

Prayer is simply talking to God, but there are several ways you can do it. The following kinds of prayer will bring variety into your conversations with God.

Praise. In praise you speak highly to God about who He is and His greatness. The focus of praise is the personhood of God. One way you can do this is by reading or quoting verses from the Book of Psalms like, "The Lord is gracious and righteous; our God is full of compassion" (Psalm 116:5).

Thanksgiving. Prayer also includes thanking God for what He has done for you and others. In fact, thanksgiving is a good way to begin your prayers. It builds your faith in what God can do for you by remembering what He has already done.

Repentance. In repentance, you admit your wrongs to God, ask for His forgiveness, and commit to turn away from sin and live the way He wants you to. Because no one is perfect and everyone makes mistakes, repentance helps us mend our relationship with God when we fail.

Petition. This means asking God to meet certain needs. Though some people never progress beyond the "gimme" stage of their prayer life, always asking God for something, there is nothing wrong with asking the Lord for His help when you need it. In fact, God strongly encourages us to come to Him with our needs.

Intercession. Sometimes you may feel the need to pray for someone else until you have the assurance that God has answered your prayer. This is intercession, one of the greatest kinds of prayer. In intercession your prayers are focused on others and their needs, rather than your own. This kind of prayer is vital for the Christian community.

Take a few moments to carefully read the Lord's Prayer in Matthew 6:9–13. See if you can identify the different kinds of prayer in this model prayer that Jesus taught His disciples.

HOW GOD ANSWERS

This is an important lesson to learn: God answers every prayer. Sometimes He says, "Yes," sometimes He says, "No," and often He says, "Wait." But time spent in prayer is never wasted. Even more than what He does *for* you, God is interested in what He can do *in* you. Prayer changes you.

PRAYING IN PUBLIC

Sooner or later, someone will ask you to lead in prayer. Don't panic. Simply remember that you're praying to the Lord, not to the people. Pray as a representative of the group and express what you think are the general desires in that meeting. Don't worry about using fancy words; just be honest, clear, and precise.

WEEK FOUR • DAY ONE
Bible Reading & Study Questions from Mark 7:1–23

1. What were the Pharisees holding on to? (Mark 7:8)

2. What was the problem with the Pharisees' observance of traditions? (Mark 7:13)

3. What things that come from within make a person "unclean"? (Mark 7:21,22)

WEEK FOUR • DAY TWO
Bible Reading & Study Questions from Mark 7:24–30

1. What nationality was the woman and where was she from? (Mark 7:26)

2. What did the woman want Jesus to do? (Mark 7:26)

3. What did Jesus do after the woman replied to
   His remark? (Mark 7:29)

WEEK FOUR ▪ DAY THREE
Bible Reading & Study Questions from Mark 7:31–37

1. Describe the method Jesus used to heal the
   deaf and mute man. (Mark 7:33)

2. What words did Jesus use when healing the
   man? (Mark 7:34)

3. What was the people's reaction after hearing
   about the healing? (Mark 7:37)

WEEK FOUR ▪ DAY FOUR
Bible Reading & Study Questions from Mark 8:1–13

1. What was Jesus' attitude toward the crowd who
   had followed Him for three days without food?
   (Mark 8:2)

2. How many loaves of bread and fish did Jesus use
   to feed the crowd? (Mark 8:5,7)

3. How many basketfuls of food were left over after everyone ate and was satisfied? (Mark 8:8)

4. How many men, besides women and children, were fed? (Mark 8:9)

5. After the miraculous feeding of the four thousand, what did the Pharisees ask Jesus for to test Him? (Mark 8:11)

WEEK FOUR • DAY FIVE
Bible Reading & Study Questions from Mark 8:14–21

1. Why did the disciples think Jesus was warning them about the yeast (teaching) of the Pharisees? (Mark 8:14,16)

2. What two miracles did Jesus use as examples to show the disciples they had misunderstood His warning? (Mark 8:19,20)

1. Describe the method Jesus used to heal the blind man. (Mark 8:23,25)

2. Rather than the healing being immediate, what was the first result? (Mark 8:24)

1. Who did Peter say Jesus was? (Mark 8:29)

2. Jesus told His followers that He must suffer, be rejected, and then be killed. What three things did Jesus say a person must do to be His follower? (Mark 8:34)

3. What did Jesus teach would happen to the people who lose their lives for Him and the gospel? (Mark 8:35)

4. What did Jesus say is worth more than all the world? (Mark 8:36)

HOW
CAN I BE
A STRONG
CHRISTIAN?

As a Christian, you need strength to overcome life's challenges and to serve the Lord effectively. You may feel inadequate on your own, but if you trust in God and not only in yourself, He will help you through any battle.

The first time you're weak and fail you may think, "It's no use. I can't live the Christian life. I might as well give up." The enemy, Satan, puts these thoughts into your mind to discourage you. You may feel defeated when you face temptation to sin—even if you don't sin. Many things in life can make you feel like a weak Christian, but here are some things you can remember to help you grow strong.

TEMPTATION IS NOT SIN

Temptation is only having the desire or pull to do something you know is wrong. Everyone has these feelings at times, but it is important not to give in to them. Jesus was tempted, but He overcame temptation by resisting it and quoting God's Word. Just like Jesus, you have the strength to overcome any temptation that comes your way!

KNOW YOUR WEAK POINTS

As a new Christian, you may still be struggling with life-controlling issues. Perhaps these are things that have a powerful grip on your life—a bad temper, addictions, or some other weakness. Knowing where you are weak will help you know how to pray for God's help. God understands and will help you overcome these challenges as you trust in Him.

COOPERATE WITH GOD

Rely on Jesus to help you overcome struggles. Jesus Christ lives in your heart through His Holy Spirit, who is called "the Comforter," meaning "one called alongside to help." The Holy Spirit will help you grow as a Christian by developing in you the nine fruit of the Spirit (see Galatians 5:22,23) that together are the character of Christ. God's purpose is to make you like Jesus. To help you better understand about the Holy Spirit, underline the things Jesus promised the Holy Spirit would do in John 14 and 16.

Having an obedient attitude to God will help you become a strong Christian. Obey the Lord when you feel Him suggesting something to you by His Holy Spirit. It is easier to be confident in your actions when you do what you believe God has told you. Also, listen to pastors and other mature Christians. They can help as well.

FOCUS ON GOD'S WORD

Memorize portions of the Bible and think about it often. The writer of the Book of Psalms wrote, "I have hidden your word in my heart that I might not sin against you" (Psalm 119:11). Knowing God's Word strengthens us so we can overcome temptation. When you feel tempted, God can help you remember Bible verses you have studied to help you resist the temptation. Here are two good verses to memorize.

"Submit yourselves, then, to God. Resist the devil, and he will flee from you" (James 4:7).

"No temptation has seized you except what is common to man. And God is faithful; he will not let you be tempted beyond what you can bear. But when you are tempted, he will also provide a way out so that you can stand up under it" (1 Corinthians 10:13).

DON'T GET DISCOURAGED

It is up to you to never give up. A baby that is starting to walk often falls, but only learns to walk by getting up and trying again. If you make a mistake and do something you know is wrong, simply come to God as you did the first time, ask Him to forgive you, and go on.

1. Which disciples did Jesus take with Him to the high mountain? (Mark 9:2)

2. What happened to Jesus' appearance when He was transfigured (transformed or changed)? (Mark 9:3)

3. What two people came and talked with Jesus during His transfiguration? (Mark 9:4)

4. What did God say about Jesus during the Transfiguration? (Mark 9:7)

1. What did Jesus say is possible for those who believe? (Mark 9:23)

2. What response did the father of the demon-possessed boy give to Jesus' statement? (Mark 9:24)

3. What did Jesus say was the reason the disciples had not been able to drive out the demon? (Mark 9:29)

4. What teaching of Jesus did the disciples not understand? (Mark 9:31)

WEEK FIVE ▪ DAY THREE
Bible Reading & Study Questions from Mark 9:33–50

1. What were the disciples arguing about? (Mark 9:34)

2. What was Jesus' response? (Mark 9:35)

3. Jesus used an illustration to help us understand the importance of eliminating things from our life that cause us to sin. What three things did Jesus use to describe the things we do, the places we go, and the things we see? (Mark 9:43–48)

WEEK FIVE • DAY FOUR
Bible Reading & Study Questions from Mark 10:1–16

1. Why did the Pharisees ask Jesus about divorce?
   (Mark 10:2)

2. Why did Jesus say divorce was allowed in the
   Old Testament law written by Moses?
   (Mark 10:5)

3. How should we come to Jesus? (Mark 10:15)

WEEK FIVE • DAY FIVE
Bible Reading & Study Questions from Mark 10:17–31

1. How did Jesus feel about the rich man?
   (Mark 10:21)

2. What did Jesus say people would receive who
   leave behind family and possessions in exchange
   for Him and the gospel? (Mark 10:30)

WEEK FIVE • DAY SIX
Bible Reading & Study Questions from Mark 10:32–45

1. What did Jesus say would happen to Him in
   Jerusalem? (Mark 10:33–34)

2. What did Jesus say a person must do to become great? (Mark 10:43)

3. What did Jesus say He ("the Son of Man") came to earth to do? (Mark 10:45)

WEEK FIVE ▪ DAY SEVEN
Bible Reading & Study Questions from Mark 10:46–52

1. What did blind Bartimaeus shout as Jesus passed by? (Mark 10:47)

2. What did Bartimaeus do as soon as Jesus sent for him? (Mark 10:50)

3. When Jesus healed Bartimaeus, what reason did Jesus give for healing him? (Mark 10:52)

4. What did Bartimaeus do after he was healed? (Mark 10:52)

WHAT DOES GOD EXPECT OF ME?

In John 16:13, it says that the Holy Spirit "will guide you into all truth." This truth includes Christian responsibilities. It's all part of growing up spiritually. In the natural, parents give their young children few responsibilities. As the child grows, more responsibilities are given. Let's talk about some spiritual responsibilities.

MAKE CHRIST THE MASTER

To express their loyalty to Jesus when He was living on earth, His disciples often called Him "Lord" or "Master." Jesus accepted this position and said, "If you love me, you will obey what I command" (John 14:15).

As a believer, you now belong to Christ because He bought you by paying for your sins when He died. Obedience shouldn't only be an obligation though. When you think about how much Jesus has done for you by dying for you and saving you from spending eternity in hell, you should be glad to show your love for Him by obeying Him.

PUT CHRIST FIRST IN YOUR LIFE

You make Jesus first in your life through developing your relationship with Him. Develop your relationship by talking to Him and listening to Him. Talk with Him through prayer—at regular times and during the day. Listen to Him through reading the Bible. Think of what you are reading as Jesus' message to you. Make Jesus the center of your life by revolving every activity in your day around how you think Jesus would act and react in the same situation.

BECOME INVOLVED IN A CHURCH

You're part of a new family—the people of God. Show that you belong to the family by being involved in a Bible-believing church. This will give you an increased sense of belonging and will provide an opportunity to help others. Being part of a church and its ministries will minister to your needs as well.

GIVE CHRIST YOUR TIME

To mature as a Christian, it is vital to give Jesus some of your time every day. You should give Him practical time in which you attend church, are involved in church activities, and help other Christians with their needs. You should also give Him personal time to develop your relationship through private devotions (Bible reading, prayer, etc.) and family devotions, if you live with Christian family members. The more time you devote to Jesus, the more you will gain in maturity and spiritual strength!

GIVE CHRIST YOUR ABILITIES

Everyone can do something. If you have special talents or abilities, use them to do the Lord's work. Besides jobs that call for special talents, there are many general tasks you can do. Your pastor and other church leaders will be happy for you to volunteer. Promise the Lord that you will try to do anything you are asked to do for Him.

GIVE CHRIST YOUR MATERIAL POSSESSIONS

Everything you possess is from God, yet He only asks for a small portion back. One important way of giving back to God is through tithing—giving 10 percent of your income to the church. Through tithes, you help support your church and spread the gospel at home and in other nations. Give offerings above your tithe for specific events and occasions. It may sound like a lot, but God will meet and exceed your needs, as you are faithful to Him.

TELL OTHERS OF YOUR FAITH

Christ commanded His disciples to tell others about what He did (Matthew 28:18–20). They told people, who told other people, who told others. The message has passed on like that for almost two thousand years. Eventually someone told you about Jesus Christ, or you would not be a Christian today.

It is now your turn to witness, or tell others about Jesus and what He has done for you. As you witness, it will become easier and more comfortable. Next to your salvation, one of your greatest thrills will be telling someone about Jesus and that person deciding to become a Christian. Make a point to talk to someone about Jesus every day.

WEEK SIX ▪ DAY ONE
Bible Reading & Study Questions from Mark 11:1–11

1. What was special about the colt Jesus sent the disciples to get? (Mark 11:2)

2. What was spread on the road in front of Jesus? (Mark 11:8)

3. What was shouted as Jesus entered Jerusalem? (Mark 11:9,10)

WEEK SIX ▪ DAY TWO
Bible Reading & Study Questions from Mark 11:12–19

1. Jesus used the fig tree as an illustration of what was lacking in the religion of His day. What did the fig tree lack? (Mark 11:13)

2. What was the temple supposed to be? (Mark 11:17)

3. What did Jesus say the temple had become? (Mark 11:17)

4. What did the religious leaders begin to do after Jesus made the statement? (Mark 11:18)

WEEK SIX • DAY THREE
Bible Reading & Study Questions from Mark 11:20–33

1. What did Jesus say we must do for our prayers to be answered? (Mark 11:22,24)

2. What did Jesus say we must do when we pray so our Heavenly Father will forgive our sins? (Mark 11:25)

3. Why did the religious leaders not want to answer Jesus' question? (Mark 11:32)

WEEK SIX • DAY FOUR
Bible Reading & Study Questions from Mark 12:1–12

1. In this parable, what did the owner of the vineyard want to happen when he sent his son to the tenants? (Mark 12:6)

2. What did the tenants hope to accomplish by killing the son? (Mark 12:7)

3. Jesus told this parable to the religious leaders of His day. The vineyard owner represents God, the servants sent to collect the fruit represent the Old Testament prophets, the son represents Jesus, and the "others" represent all who will accept Jesus as Savior. Who do the tenants represent? (Mark 12:12)

WEEK SIX • DAY FIVE
Bible Reading & Study Questions from Mark 12:13–17

1. Trying to flatter Jesus, the religious leaders made some key observations about Him. What were their observations? (Mark 12:14)

2. What did the religious leaders ask Jesus to trick Him so that the Roman government would have grounds to arrest Him? (Mark 12:14,15)

3. What did Jesus perceive about the religious leaders? (Mark 12:15)

4. What was their reaction to Jesus' answer? (Mark 12:17)

WEEK SIX • DAY SIX
Bible Reading & Study Questions from Mark 12:18–34

1. What was the Sadducees' question? (Mark 12:23)

2. Before we can understand Jesus' response to the Sadducees, what should we know about their beliefs? (Mark 12:18)

3. Why did Jesus say the Sadducees were in error for not believing in the resurrection (eternal life in heaven)? (Mark 12:24)

4. What did Jesus say are the two greatest commandments? (Mark 12:30,31)

1. What was the crowd's reaction to Jesus' teaching? (Mark 12:37)

2. What will happen to people who only practice an outward religion? (Mark 12:40)

3. Why did Jesus say the poor widow had given more than all the others at the temple? (Mark 12:44)

HOW CAN I KNOW THE WILL OF GOD?

How to know the will of God—that's a big enough subject to write volumes on. Yet it is something important for every Christian to know and pursue. After all, since Christ is now your Master and you want to obey Him, you must learn what He wants you to do with your life.

WHEN IT'S A MATTER OF CONDUCT

Everyone knows there is a difference between right and wrong, even people who have never heard of God's law or read the Bible. Jesus taught that the two most important commandments are to love God and to love our neighbor the way we love ourselves (Mark 12:28–31). The second of these commandments means that we should act toward others as we want them to act toward us. This law has become known as "the Golden Rule." Obedience to these two laws is the first step of living in God's will.

You are now Jesus' representative in the world. In deciding how you should live, be guided by your love for Jesus. That love will lead you to a life that glorifies God. When you have an important decision to make, ask yourself, "What can I do that would best please Jesus?" If that is the ruling question in your decisions, you will make the right choice.

WHEN YOU MUST DECIDE WHICH WAY TO GO

Sometimes we must choose how to act from among several options—all of which could please God. How can you decide which is best?

Be patient. Learn to wait on God until He indicates His will to you. Time has a way of working things out. Don't be in a hurry.

Seek the advice of others. Don't be a loner. Let your pastor or another mature Christian help you. Be sure it is someone who will keep your confidence. Someone who is not directly involved in your situation can often see things more clearly than you can.

Commit the matter to the Lord. A famous Christian, George Müller, used this method: He would list the reasons for and against a certain course of action and prayerfully consider the matter for a time. Then he would decide to move in a certain direction. He would remove from his mind as much of his own desires as possible, and then ask God to block his path if it were not His will. Over a period of fifty years Müller found this approach successful.

GETTING ALONG WITH OTHERS

It is God's will that you treat everyone in love, whether it is easy or not. If you haven't learned this yet, you will soon discover that no one is perfect and even Christians can be hard to get along with sometimes. Just like you, God is trying to work in their lives to make them more like Jesus.

You will naturally be drawn to make certain Christians close friends. Other Christians may be a challenge to be friendly with. Remember that we all have traits that others may find annoying, but God wants all Christians to treat each other like brothers and sisters in a loving family.

The most important gift you can ask for from God is the ability to love Him and others at all times. This love is vital because it causes you to develop all the traits God wants you to have. Love will make you want a close relationship with God. Love will make you considerate of others. Love will make you want to witness to others. Love can even help you accept those who seem impossible.

WEEK SEVEN · DAY ONE
Bible Reading & Study Questions from Mark 13:1–23

1. What did Jesus say about the stones of the temple? (Mark 13:2)

2. List four end-time signs that Jesus described as the "beginning of birth pains." (Mark 13:5–8)

3. What will happen to one who "stands firm till the end" in the time of persecution? (Mark 13:13)

4. What does Jesus tell us to do in response to His warnings about the end-time? (Mark 13:23)

WEEK SEVEN · DAY TWO
Bible Reading & Study Questions from Mark 13:24–37

1. What will happen when we see Jesus coming in the clouds? (Mark 13:27)

2. What will never pass away? (Mark 13:31)

3. Who knows the day and hour of Christ's return? (Mark 13:32)

4. What does Jesus tell us to do to prepare for His return? (Mark 13:33,37)

WEEK SEVEN ▪ DAY THREE
Bible Reading & Study Questions from Mark 14:1–11

1. What did the woman do with the alabaster jar filled with expensive perfume? (Mark 14:3)

2. What was the reaction of the people who saw her do this? (Mark 14:5)

3. What did Jesus say was the purpose of her action? (Mark 14:8)

4. What did Judas Iscariot do after this event? (Mark 14:10,11)

WEEK SEVEN ▪ DAY FOUR
Bible Reading & Study Questions from Mark 14:12–31

1. What did Jesus compare the broken bread to? (Mark 14:22)

2. What did Jesus compare the cup to? (Mark 14:23,24)

3. Who is Jesus' blood poured out for? (Mark 14:24)

4. What was Jesus' prediction about Peter?
(Mark 14:30)

WEEK SEVEN • DAY FIVE
Bible Reading & Study Questions from Mark 14:32–52

1. What did Jesus say is possible for God to do?
(Mark 14:36)

2. Whose will did Jesus pray would be done?
(Mark 14:36)

3. Why did Jesus tell Peter that he should continue
to watch and pray? (Mark 14:38)

4. What happened to Jesus' followers when He was
arrested? (Mark 14:50)

WEEK SEVEN • DAY SIX
Bible Reading & Study Questions from Mark 14:53–65

1. Who followed at a distance when Jesus was
taken for trial before the religious leaders?
(Mark 14:54)

2. What were the religious leaders looking for?
(Mark 14:55)

3. What was Jesus' reaction to the false accusations against Him? (Mark 14:61)

4. When the high priest asked Jesus if He was the Christ, what did Jesus say? (Mark 14:62)

WEEK SEVEN · DAY SEVEN
Bible Reading & Study Questions from Mark 14:66–72

1. How many times did Peter deny knowing Jesus? (Mark 14:68,70,71)

2. What happened after Peter's third denial? (Mark 14:72)

3. What was Peter's reaction as soon as he remembered Jesus' prophecy about his denial? (Mark 14:72)

WHAT ARE THE TWO BAPTISMS?

By now you probably realize that salvation is just the first step in your spiritual life as a Christian. There are many other important steps you should take. Two of these important steps are the two baptisms.

WATER BAPTISM

One of the most important things you can do in your new life is to follow Jesus' example of water baptism. Water baptism is a way of showing others that you have given your life to Jesus.

The Greek word for baptism is *baptizō*, which means immerse. When you are baptized in water, you will be immersed—put completely under the water. When you go down into the water, it symbolizes Jesus' death and burial, and that your old, sinful life is dead and buried. When you come out of the water, it symbolizes Jesus' resurrection and your new life in Him.

Water baptism is also an act of obedience. After His resurrection, Jesus commanded, "Go and make disciples of all nations, baptizing them in the name of the Father and of the Son and of the Holy Spirit" (Matthew 28:19). As you daily surrender your life to Jesus and become more like Him, He expects that you will obey Him. Water baptism is a first step in being obedient to Jesus.

If you were baptized as a baby, you might wonder if you need to be baptized again. The Bible instructs that water baptism is for anyone who has recognized the need of a Savior, has repented, and believed in Christ (Acts 2:38,41; 8:36–38). Because a baby is unable to repent of sin and accept Christ as Savior, that person should be baptized in water after becoming a Christian.

You should be baptized as soon as possible. Talk to your pastor this week about setting a date and time.

HOLY SPIRIT BAPTISM

To understand the baptism in the Holy Spirit, you need to understand who the Holy Spirit is. He is the Third Person of the Trinity. *Trinity* is a term used to describe the one true and living God, manifested in three Persons: God the Father, God the Son, and God the Holy Spirit. The Father, Son, and Holy Spirit are distinct Persons, and each is God—not three gods, but one God in three Persons.

God the Father is your Creator, maker of the universe, and the giver of all life.

God the Son (Jesus Christ) is your Savior who became a man to show the world what God is like. He paid the penalty for your sin and has provided everlasting life to anyone who will receive Him.

God the Holy Spirit is your Helper who assists you in receiving God's forgiveness and obeying Him. The Holy Spirit also gives you power to live like Jesus and to tell others about Him.

When you became a Christian, the Holy Spirit came to live in you. He lives in each Christian to help that person live a life that pleases God and is full of joy. The Holy Spirit lets you know when you sin and gives you power to overcome temptation. The Holy Spirit also helps you understand, learn, and remember Scripture. He is your guide, comforter, helper, and teacher.

Although the Holy Spirit already lives inside you, the baptism in the Holy Spirit brings His power in your life to another level. To better understand the baptism in the Holy Spirit, compare it to water baptism. Just as water baptism means to be immersed in water, being baptized in the Holy Spirit means to be immersed in the Holy Spirit. The Holy Spirit completely fills you in a greater way than before.

Before His return to heaven, Jesus said,

> Do not leave Jerusalem, but wait for the gift
> my Father promised, which you have heard
> me speak about. For John baptized with
> water, but in a few days you will be baptized
> with the Holy Spirit. . . . You will receive
> power when the Holy Spirit comes on you;
> and you will be my witnesses in Jerusalem,
> and in all Judea and Samaria, and to the ends
> of the earth (Acts 1:4–5,8).

The next chapter of the Book of Acts records
the coming of this promised gift on the Day of
Pentecost. In your Bible, read Acts 2:1–8, 11–18.

Jesus' closest followers were baptized in the Holy
Spirit and began speaking in languages they had
never learned! We call these other languages
"tongues." Speaking in tongues is the initial
physical evidence, or proof, of being baptized in
the Holy Spirit (Acts 2:4; 10:46; 19:6).

Not only is speaking in tongues part of the initial
experience of being baptized in the Holy Spirit,
it is also a continual part of a Christian's private
prayer life (1 Corinthians 14:2). God directs us to
pray in tongues when we do not know how to
pray for a specific issue. "The Spirit helps us in our
weakness. We do not know what we ought to pray

for, but the Spirit himself intercedes for us with groans that words cannot express" (Romans 8:26).

You need the Holy Spirit's help just as Jesus' first followers did. The Holy Spirit will be your help as He gives you the power and ability to be a witness for Jesus Christ, both in what you do and what you say.

Ask Jesus to baptize you in the Holy Spirit, believe that He will, and wait patiently. It is a gift (Acts 1:4) and a promise: "The promise is for you and your children and for all who are far off—for all whom the Lord our God will call" (Acts 2:39). Ask your pastor or a Christian friend for more information on how to receive this gift from God.

The baptism in the Holy Spirit is not a once-for-all experience. As you continue to stay close to the Lord in prayer and reading His Word, the Holy Spirit will work in you more and more.

WEEK EIGHT ▪ DAY ONE
Bible Reading & Study Questions from Mark 15:1–15

1. Because the religious leaders did not have the authority to sentence Jesus to death they took Him to Pilate, the Roman ruler for that region. What was Pilate's reaction when Jesus gave no response to the false accusations against Him? (Mark 15:5)

2. What was the custom at the Feast of Unleavened Bread? (Mark 15:6)

3. Why did Pilate offer to release Jesus? (Mark 15:10)

4. Why did Pilate agree to release Barabbas and have Jesus flogged and crucified? (Mark 15:15)

WEEK EIGHT · DAY TWO
Bible Reading & Study Questions from Mark 15:16–20

1. What piece of clothing did the Roman soldiers put on Jesus to mock Him? (Mark 15:17)

2. What did they place on Jesus' head? (Mark 15:17)

3. What did they call out to Jesus? (Mark 15:18)

4. The soldiers spit on Jesus and struck Him on the head with what? (Mark 15:19)

1. What was Simon from Cyrene forced to do? (Mark 15:21)

2. Where was Jesus crucified and what did the place's name mean? (Mark 15:22)

3. Who was crucified with Jesus? (Mark 15:27)

4. Name three groups of people who insulted or mocked Jesus as He hung on the cross. (Mark 15:29,31,32)

1. What happened from the sixth hour until the ninth hour on the day Jesus was crucified? (Mark 15:33)

2. What did Jesus cry out at the ninth hour? (Mark 15:34)

3. What happened immediately after Jesus died? (Mark 15:38)

4. What was the reaction of the centurion, the Roman solider who oversaw Jesus' crucifixion, after Jesus died? (Mark 15:39)

WEEK EIGHT • DAY FIVE
Bible Reading & Study Questions from Mark 15:42–47

1. Who requested Jesus' body to prepare it for burial? (Mark 15:43)

2. Who verified for Pilate that Jesus had already died? (Mark 15:45)

3. List the steps Joseph took to bury Jesus. (Mark 15:46)

WEEK EIGHT • DAY SIX
Bible Reading & Study Questions from Mark 16:1–8

1. What were the women wondering on their way to the tomb early on Sunday morning? (Mark 16:2,3)

2. What did they see when they got there? (Mark 16:4)

3. Describe the angel that the women saw when they entered the tomb. (Mark 16:5)

4. What did the angel say to them? (Mark 16:6,7)

WEEK EIGHT · DAY SEVEN
Bible Reading & Study Questions from Mark 16:9–20

1. List three people or groups of people Jesus appeared to following His resurrection. (Mark 16:9,12,14)

2. What did Jesus command His followers to do? (Mark 16:15)

3. What will happen to the people who believe the good news and are baptized? (Mark 16:16)

4. What will happen to the people who do not believe the good news? (Mark 16:16)

5. What did Jesus' disciples do after Jesus was taken up into heaven? (Mark 16:20)

6. Who worked with Jesus' followers when they preached and how was the message proven? (Mark 16:20)

WHAT NOW?

Well, the first eight weeks are over. How did you do? Now, what about the future? Let's reemphasize some points and consider a few reminders and tips.

BIBLE READING

Read the Bible every day for at least fifteen minutes. Read the Gospel of Mark through two more times, then start at Matthew and read through the Book of Acts. Move to the first book in the Bible, Genesis, and read it next. Go back and read the New Testament all the way through. Then ask your pastor for a daily Bible reading plan.

As you continue to grow as a Christian, daily Bible reading is one of the most important steps you can take.

PRAYER

Prayer is the lifeline of your spiritual life. Think of God as a best friend you can confide in. Talk to Him daily about your victories as well as your needs.

FIND A CHURCH HOME

Become involved in a good church, attend regularly, and help in every way possible.

BE BAPTIZED IN WATER

The Lord has commanded water baptism. It is one of the ways you can give a public testimony of your salvation and relationship with Jesus.

THE BAPTISM IN THE HOLY SPIRIT

Actively pray to be baptized in the Holy Spirit. He is your Counselor and Friend who is there to help you.

BECOME A GIVER

Give ten cents out of every dollar you earn to the church you have made your church home. This is known as the tithe. Then give offerings as the Lord blesses you and impresses on your heart to give above your tithe.

WHEN YOU FAIL

When you fail, ask God for forgiveness, just as you did the first time. He will never give up on you. But determine by His help not to fail in the same way again.

WHAT NOW?

It depends on you. By following these suggestions, you will begin to grow as a Christian and mature spiritually.

PATTERN FOR BIBLE STUDY

When you study the Bible, use the following questions to help you.

INTENT
What does this passage say and really mean?

DIFFICULTY
What does it say that I don't understand?

COMPARISON
What similar thoughts are found elsewhere in the Bible?

PROMISES
What blessings are stated that are for all believers?

WARNINGS
What warnings apply to my everyday life?

COMMANDS
What commands should I obey?

WEEKLY PRAYER GUIDE

Make it a habit to pray every day. Use the following prayer guide as a suggested direction for your daily, dedicated prayer time.

SUNDAY

S is for Sinners; pray especially that God will reach those who don't know Christ through the church services.

MONDAY

M is for Missionaries; pray for those who go to places other than their home to spread the message of Jesus.

TUESDAY

T is for Tasks; pray about your particular work for God.

WEDNESDAY

W is for Workers; pray for the pastor and others who work in your church.

THURSDAY

T is for Thanksgiving; express gratitude for what God has done for you and others.

FRIDAY

F is for Families and Friends; pray for their salvation if they are not saved and that they will continue to grow closer to Christ.

SATURDAY

S is for Saints, fellow believers; pray that they will grow into mature believers.

SUGGESTED MEMORY VERSES (BY TOPIC)

COMMUNION
1 Corinthians 11:26

END-TIME
John 14:2,3
Acts 1:11
1 Corinthians 15:52
1 Thessalonians 4:16,17
Titus 2:13

FAITH
John 20:29
2 Corinthians 5:7
Ephesians 2:8
2 Timothy 1:12
Hebrews 11:1
Hebrews 11:6

GIVING/MONEY
Matthew 6:24
Luke 6:38
2 Corinthians 9:6,7
Philippians 4:11
1 Timothy 6:9,10

GOD
Genesis 1:1
Genesis 1:27
Exodus 20:7
Deuteronomy 6:4

GOD'S WORD
Deuteronomy 6:6–9
Joshua 1:8
Psalm 1:2,3
Psalm 119:11
Psalm 119:105
Matthew 5:17,18
Matthew 24:35
John 1:1
John 15:7
Acts 17:11
Romans 1:16
Romans 10:17
1 Thessalonians 2:13
2 Timothy 2:15
2 Timothy 3:14–17
Hebrews 4:12

GUIDANCE
Psalm 16:11
Psalm 37:4
Proverbs 3:5,6
Proverbs 16:9

HEALING
Isaiah 53:5
Acts 3:6
James 5:14–16

HOLY LIVING
Deuteronomy 6:25
Psalm 24:3,4
Psalm 119:3
John 14:15
John 15:10
Acts 24:16
Philippians 1:9–11
Philippians 2:3
Philippians 4:9
Colossians 3:9,10
1 Thessalonians 5:23
Hebrews 12:14
1 Peter 1:15,16

HOLY SPIRIT
Acts 1:4,5
Acts 1:8
Acts 2:4
Acts 2:38,39
Acts 4:31
Galatians 5:22,23

JESUS CHRIST
Matthew 1:23
Matthew 16:16
Matthew 28:6
Luke 1:35
Luke 3:22
John 1:3
2 Corinthians 5:21
Philippians 2:9–11
Hebrews 7:23–28
Hebrews 13:8
1 Peter 2:22
Revelation 22:13

LOVE
Matthew 5:44
Luke 10:27
John 13:35
John 15:13
1 Corinthians 13
Ephesians 3:17–19
Hebrews 10:24
1 John 4:8
1 John 4:20

MINISTRY
Matthew 5:16
Mark 16:15
Hebrews 10:25
1 Peter 3:15
1 Peter 4:10

PEACE
Psalm 4:8
John 14:27
John 16:33
Romans 5:1
Philippians 4:7

PRAYER
Matthew 6:9–13
Matthew 21:22
1 Thessalonians 5:17

SALVATION
Proverbs 28:13
Luke 19:10
John 1:11,12
John 1:29
John 3:3
John 3:16,17
John 6:35
John 10:10
John 11:25
John 14:6
John 20:31
Acts 4:12
Acts 16:31
Romans 1:16
Romans 5:8
Romans 6:23
Romans 10:9
Romans 12:1,2
2 Corinthians 5:17
Galatians 2:20
Ephesians 2:8
James 1:22
2 Peter 1:20,21
1 John 1:9
1 John 4:9
Revelation 1:3

TEMPTATIONS AND TRIALS
Genesis 4:7
Matthew 26:41
1 Corinthians 10:13
Ephesians 6:10–18
James 1:2–4
James 1:12

THANKFULNESS
Psalm 136:1
Colossians 3:17
1 Thessalonians 5:18

WATER BAPTISM
Matthew 28:19
Romans 6:4

NOTES

NOTES

NOTES

NOTES

NOTES

NOTES

NOTES

NOTES

NOTES

NOTES